BELLWETHER MEDIA • MINNEAPOLIS, MN

BLASTOFF! READERS

by Shannon Anderson

Chile

COUNTRIES OF THE WORLD

WELCOME TO CHILE

Printed in the United States of America, North Mankato, MN.

Editor: Rachael Barnes   Series Design: Gabriel Hilger   Book Designer: Kathleen Petelinsek

Text copyright © 2024 by Bellwether Media, Inc. BLASTOFF! READERS and associated logos are trademarks and/or registered trademarks of Bellwether Media, Inc.

LC record available at https://lccn.loc.gov/2023046604
LC ebook record available at https://lccn.loc.gov/2023046605

Classification: LCC F3058.5 .A54 2024 (print) | LCC F3058.5 (ebook) | DDC 983–dc23/eng/20231018
Subjects: LCSH: Chile—Juvenile literature.
ISBN 9798886877851 (ebook)
Identifiers: LCCN 2023046604 (print) | LCCN 2023046605 (ebook) | ISBN 9798886877915 (library binding) |
Provided by publisher.
Includes bibliographical references and index. | Audience: Ages 5–8 | Audience: Grades 2–3 | Summary: "Relevant images match informative text in this introduction to Chile. Intended for students in kindergarten through third grade"—
Description: Minneapolis, MN : Bellweather Media, Inc., 2024. | Series: Blastoff! Readers : Countries of the world |
Title: Chile / by Shannon Anderson.
Names: Anderson, Shannon, 1972- author.

Library of Congress Cataloging-in-Publication Data

6012 Blue Circle Drive, Minnetonka, MN 55343.
For information regarding permission, write to Bellwether Media, Inc., Attention: Permissions Department,
No part of this publication may be reproduced in whole or in part without written permission of the publisher.

This edition first published in 2024 by Bellwether Media, Inc.

Reading Level

Grade K — Blastoff! Beginners
Grades 1–3 — Blastoff! Readers
Grade 4 — Blastoff! Discovery

★ Blastoff! Universe

 **Level 1** provides the most support through repetition of high-frequency words, light text, predictable sentence patterns, and strong visual support.

 **Level 2** offers early readers a bit more challenge through varied sentences, increased text load, and text-supportive special features.

 **Level 3** advances early-fluent readers toward fluency through increased text load, less reliance on photos, advancing concepts, longer sentences, and more complex special features.

Blastoff! Readers are carefully developed by literacy experts to build reading stamina and move students toward fluency by combining standards-based content with developmentally appropriate text.

Table of Contents

All About Chile 4
Land and Animals 6
Life in Chile 12
Chile Facts 20
Glossary 22
To Learn More 23
Index 24

All About Chile

Chile is in South America. Its capital is Santiago.

Santiago

Chile is the narrowest country in the world! The Pacific Ocean meets its long western coast.

Land and Animals

The Andes Mountains stand in the east. Many of the mountains are **volcanoes**! A dry **desert** fills the north. Rivers flow through central Chile. **Glaciers** sit in the south.

desert

9

Nevados Ojos del Salado

Size: 22,569 feet (6,879 meters) tall
Famous For: the world's tallest active volcano

Most of Chile has a mild **climate**. The mountains are cooler.

Andes Mountains

Northern Chile is often foggy. Southern Chile gets the most rain.

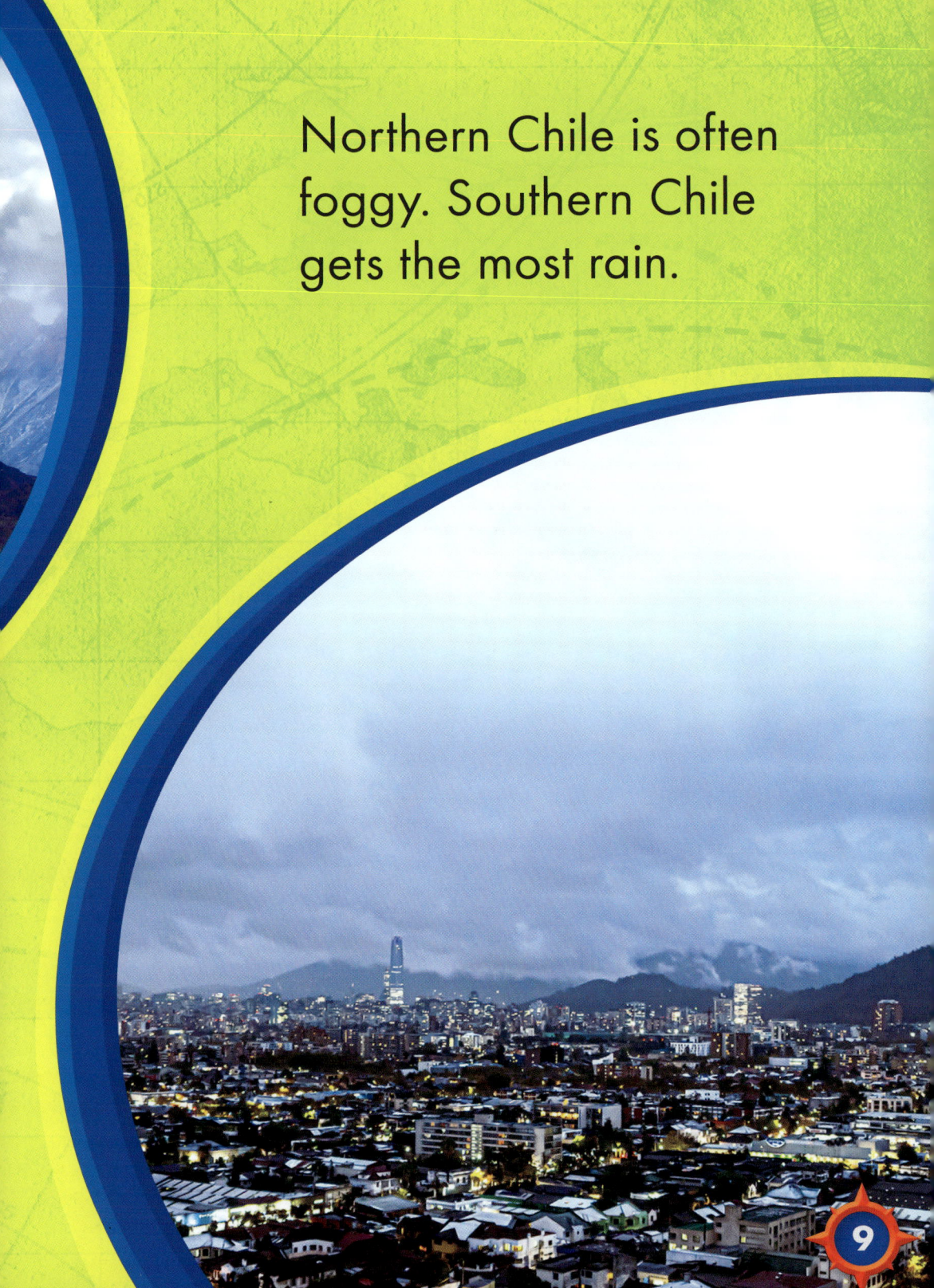

huemul

Many animals call the mountains home. Huemul **herds** eat plants in the south. Pumas hunt the herds.

Chinchillas live between mountain rocks. Andean condors fly overhead.

Animals of Chile

chinchilla

Andean condor

huemul

puma

Catholic church in Santiago

Life in Chile

Most Chileans live in cities. They speak Spanish.

Over half of the people in Chile are **Catholics**. Many people have a European background.

Many famous poets are from Chile. Chileans also enjoy concerts and **folk music**.

folk music

rodeo

soccer

Soccer is a popular sport. Some Chileans go to the **rodeo**. Others visit the beach.

Chilean Foods

empanadas

alfajores

pastel de choclo

cazuela

Pastel de choclo is a popular meat and corn dish. *Cazuela* is a favorite meat and vegetable stew.

Empanadas are filled pastries. Sandwich cookies called *alfajores* are sweet treats!

making alfajores

Independence Day in Chile is September 18. People eat, dance, and gather in parks.

Independence Day

Families share a late-night meal on Christmas Eve. Chilean holidays bring people together!

Chile Facts

Size: 291,933 square miles (756,103 square kilometers)

Population: 18,549,457 (2023)

National Holiday: Independence Day (September 18)

Main Language: Spanish

Capital City: Santiago

Famous Face

Name: Michelle Bachelet
Famous For: first woman president of Chile

20

Top Landmarks

Torres del Paine National Park

Hand of the Desert

Easter Island

Religions

- Roman Catholic 60%
- Evangelical 18%
- none 17%
- other 5%

Glossary

Catholics—people belonging to or relating to the Christian church that is led by the pope

climate—the usual weather conditions of a place

desert—dry land with few plants and little rainfall

folk music—the traditional music of the people in a country or region

glaciers—massive sheets of ice that cover large areas of land

herds—groups of animals that live and travel together

rodeo—a show in which riders perform certain skills on horses

volcanoes—holes in the earth, when a volcano erupts, hot ash, gas, or melted rock called lava shoots out.

To Learn More

AT THE LIBRARY

Blake, Kevin. *Chile*. New York, N.Y.: Bearport Publishing, 2020.

Riggs, Kate. *Cougars*. Mankato, Minn.: Creative Education, 2022.

Spanier, Kristine. *Easter Island*. Minneapolis, Minn.: Jump!, 2022.

ON THE WEB

Factsurfer.com gives you a safe, fun way to find more information.

1. Go to www.factsurfer.com.
2. Enter "Chile" into the search box and click Q.
3. Select your book cover to see a list of related content.

Index

Andes Mountains, 6, 8, 10, 11
animals, 10, 11
beach, 15
capital (see Santiago)
Catholics, 12
Chile facts, 20-21
Christmas Eve, 19
cities, 12
climate, 8
coast, 5
concerts, 14
desert, 6
foggy, 9
folk music, 14
food, 16, 17
glaciers, 6
Independence Day, 18, 19
map, 5
Nevados Ojos del Salado, 7

Pacific Ocean, 5
people, 12, 14, 15, 18, 19
poets, 14
rain, 9
rivers, 6
rodeo, 15
Santiago, 4, 5, 12
say hello, 13
soccer, 15
South America, 4
Spanish, 12, 13
volcanoes, 6, 7

The images in this book are reproduced through the courtesy of: JVEPhoto; front cover: SL-Photography, pp. 2-3; railway fx, p. 3 (flag); Jose Luis Stephens, pp. 4-5; sunsinger, p. 6; Oliclimb, pp. 6-7; kavram, pp. 8-9; Angel Gruber, p. 9; liyenne cavalheiro, pp. 10-11; Gonzalo Garin, p. 11 (huemul); Risto Raunio, p. 11 (puma); Erhantz P.R, p. 11 (chinchilla); Don Mammoser, p. 11 (Andean condor); Diego Grandi, p. 12, mikecranephotography.com/ Alamy, pp. 12-13; Solucionfotografica, pp. 14-15; Amp, p. 15 (soccer); Marcelo Vildosola Garrigo, p. 15 (rodeo); AS Foodstudio, p. 16 (pastel de choclo); Ilaii Papp, p. 16 (cazuela); hiphoto, p. 16 (empanadas); rontav, p. 16 (alfajores); Guillermo Spelucin R, p. 17; Jeremy Richards, pp. 18-19, fifoOnz, p. 20 (flag); Gobierno de Chile/ Wiki Commons, p. 20 (Michelle Bachelet); Carlos Aranguiz, p. 21 (Easter Island); Elena Chikanova, p. 21 (Hand of the Desert); ecsik22, p. 21 (Torres del Paine National Park); Evgeniyqw, p. 22.